I've Finished My Novel Now What?

Donovan M. Neal

Tornveil

Torn**Veil**

For permission requests, write to the publisher, addressed "Attention: Permissions Coordinator," at the email below.

Tornveil@donovanmneal.comISBN 978-0-9894805-5-0 (print version)

Printed in the United States of America

Contents

Preface

When I wrote this book, it was the result of having spent large amounts of time, energy, and money to get my first novel to market. I learned so much, experienced so much, and made so many mistakes that I simply did not feel other writers needed to go through the unnecessary learning curve I did. Thus, the reason for this book.

Second, I found in my personal experience that there was a lot of information about how to write: information that talked about how to put together a good plot, great dialog, how to do fight scenes, etc. However, what do you do after you have finished writing that first draft? This book is a primer for those who have done that or at least have a work in progress and want to know what to do afterward.

Third, I have had many associates and friends who have published using certain methods and have seen and heard horror stories as they have watched their works languish in the void of obscurity. This ought not to be.

This book is from a fellow author who is not so far removed from you as a writer. I am where you can be within a couple of months or a year. I am not a million-dollar seller, but I am moving closer to an enviable position in making a living with my writing. For me, it is not about whether I will make a living with my writing, but when. I am the author who started probably just like you and has learned enough to intelligently write about things so that you, too, can at least successfully launch and begin your journey. I am a touchable author who is still learning and is going to give a simple answer to your questions.

I have talked with dozens of people who aspire to write a book. I always tell them to go for it. I believe that there is a market for who we are: that there are people who need exactly the gift and talent that is resident within you and that we are the answer to someone's prayers; having said that: there is also some great works out there that I must highly recommend as required reading for the budding Authorpreneur.

I would like to think of my book like an authorprenuer's Elements of Style, yet I would be remiss not to mention the various other books that delve deeper into some of the subjects I am going to discuss. Thus, I have included a listing of recommended readings I consider must-reads for authors. With that in mind, I have tried to create a simple book that will allow you to jump right into the meat of issues without all of the fluff.

Overall, I hope that this work will help clear away some of the publishing fog of war some authors have, especially about the subject of marketing.

With those thoughts in mind, I commit this work to you and trust that you will find the information useful.

Donovan

Why another book on "self" publishing?

W hen I wrote this book, it was the result of having spent large amounts of time, energy, and money to get my first novel to market. I learned so much, experienced so much, and made so many mistakes that I simply did not feel other writers needed to go through the unnecessary learning curve I did. Thus, the reason for this book.

Second, I found in my personal experience that there was a lot of information about how to write: information that talked about how to put together a good plot, great dialog, how to do fight scenes, etc. However, what do you do after you have finished writing that first draft? This book is a primer for those who have done that or at least have a work in progress and want to know what to do afterward.

Third, I have had so many associates and friends who have published using certain methods and have seen and heard the horror stories as they have watched their works languish in the void of obscurity. This ought not to be.

This book is from a fellow author who is not so far removed from you as a writer. I am where you can be within a couple of months or a year. I am not a million-dollar seller, but I am moving closer to an enviable position in making a living with my writing. For me, it is not about whether I will make a living with my writing, but when. I am the author who started probably just like you and has learned enough to intelligently write about things so that you, too, can at least successfully launch and begin your journey. I am a touchable author who is still learning and is going to give a simple answer to your questions.

I have talked with dozens of people who aspire to write a book. I always tell them to go for it. I believe that there is a market for who we are: that there are people who need exactly the gift and talent that is resident within you and that we are the answer to someone's prayers; having said that: there is also some great works out there that I must highly recommend as required reading for the budding Authorpreneur.

I would like to think of my book like an authorprenuer's Elements of Style, yet I would be remiss not to mention the various other books that delve deeper into some of the subjects I am going to discuss. Thus, I have included a listing of recommended readings I consider must-reads for authors. With that in mind, I have tried to create a simple book that will allow you to jump right into the meat of issues without all of the fluff.

Overall, I hope that this work will help clear away some of the publishing fog of war some authors have, especially about the subject of marketing.

With those thoughts in mind, I commit this work to you and trust that you will find the information useful.

Donovan

My secret sauce to successfully publishing is something that I discovered while doing the work of getting my own book to market, failing, reading others works, and distilling into a working plan what I have seen and read what other successful authors do. Therefore, I am going to tell you right up front what you need to do to succeed, and then I am going to elaborate on each point moving forward in this book. The graphic below depicts what every author needs to do. I introduce to you the ARC. No, not Iron Man's self-sustaining reactor in the movies, but what I call Author Resource Circles.

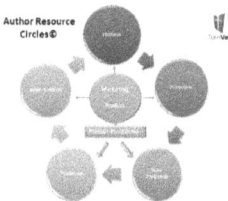

There are six areas that an author must become adept at. Each circle represents a different aspect of the publishing business that you, as an author, must become well versed in; if you wish to see any level of financial success.

The ARC comprises two sets of rings: an inner ring and an outer ring. There is the inner ring which comprises the orange circle, and the outer ring which comprises the other five. Imagine each circle as an engine that you must start. (If you have ever had to start a pull lawn mower, you are getting the idea here.) The more engines that are running, the faster you will go. Basically, the more you become proficient and expand your efforts in each circle, the more sales you should expect to make.

If you are having difficulty in selling books, simply identify which portion of the diagram needs development. This will typically pinpoint for you exactly what the problem is, and where you should direct your business efforts. Let me say this. If you are NOT selling your book, it is because somewhere on this diagram there is a broken circle. I guarantee it.

Every author starts in the same place, the center of the diagram. This circle starts with you creating a compelling and quality written product that appeals to a specific market. This is the essence of the orange circle. Fail here and the rest of the diagram does not matter. This circle represents writing a good book that has been properly edited, laid out correctly, and given a stunning professional looking cover. It means you know who your target audience is; where they congregate, and the methods used to best connect with them. This is the heart of the ARC. It is the beating heart that touches all the other circles and will help drive your efforts going forward.

After successfully developing your product and gaining an understanding of who your target demographic is; you will move from this center and determine where and how to place your product.

Product placement deals with how to distribute your product, why are you distributing your product, and the publishing model used to distribute it. (I.e., Vanity, hybrid, traditional, or independent distribution) The question of how to distribute your novel is a question that every author must answer. It means also understanding where to properly place your book in the BISAC (Book Industry Study Group) subject codes categories that best represent it. (i.e., sci-fi, romance, fantasy, high fantasy, etc.) In addition, one must know how to use keywords to get your book the most discoverability on your retailer's digital bookshelf. I have seen many authors fail before they even get into the outer ring because they make a misstep here.

Once you complete this step, you are now in the outer ring of the author resource circles (ARC). Most authors will typically begin in the traditional distribution market. This olive circle represents all the traditional formats and includes print, eBooks, libraries, audiobooks, overseas sales, and foreign language translations, to name a few.

The Outer Circle

The green circle represents all the various paid advertisements available to help increase the discoverability of your book. This includes paid email lists like Bookbub, targeted ads, paid press releases, Ad copy, book descriptions, etc.

The red circle is the platform circle. This sphere encompasses things like having an email list, a website, a robust social media presence, etc.

The rust circle comprises all non-paid discovery options. Things like book reviews, using internet radio, free giveaways, blog tours, etc.

The gold circle is usually the last circle that authors will enter. Here we are talking about non-traditional distribution like specialty shops, prisons, airports, mass merchandisers, etc.

Now keep in mind that the outer circles are not in any order. You can focus your efforts on just one or all. However, realize that the more you operate in each sphere, the more sales you will see. The more your efforts in each are habitual and systematic in your implementation, the more sales you will see.

Now what matters as it relates to the rest of the circles is not the order that you do them, but how proficient you are in each. You might find that occasionally you are spending more time developing one circle over another. Do not let that bother you, what matters most is that you are ever expanding your presence or developing a foothold in each circle, and you are actively doing something in each. As you become proficient in one area of the circle, expand to another tactic within the same circle until you feel you have a command of that circle. Do not worry about where you start: worry about *not* starting. While I typically recommend that beginning authors start with the platform circle or the promotion circle. I've observed that authors who have a command of these two will naturally focus their efforts into the others.

Remember that successful authors make sure they are moving effectively in all the circles, the more you become proficient in each one. The better results you will observe. Using this method, you can actually "track" your favorite author and study how they are using these methods.

I too can look at an author's work, or have them explain to me a problem and with this diagram see not just where the problem is, but present a workable solution to fix it. I hope this small work will help you do the same in your publishing efforts.

Remember, it all begins with the inner circle of creating a great product that targets a specific audience. Once that inner circle is mastered, then you are free to move to the outer circles. Remember that where you start is not as important as actually starting, and that you make it a point to rev each wheel in the circle. Doing so will speed you on your way.

Let us take the time to explore this concept more in-depth.

Types of Publication Options

If you are interested in publishing a novel, there are essentially three main publishing options available. I will not take much time going through them. There is plenty of information out on the internet that can give you more in-depth information about each publishing option. However, I want to review them briefly.

The three main publishing options currently available to authors at the moment are vanity press publishing, traditional publishing, and independent publishing. There is actually a new form of publishing called hybrid publishing that has materialized. Allow me to give you a quick rundown of each.

Vanity Press (You pay)

When we talk about vanity publishing, what we are talking about is a publishing option where *you* pay a publisher to publish your book for you. This usually means that you pay them an up front flat fee to do cover design, editing, proofing, typesetting, marketing, etc. I call this the "book in a box" method.

This option caters to persons who have resources, and will make what is typically a heavy financial investment, and assume all the financial risk. (Often unknowingly.) Persons who use this method either desire little control over the publishing process or have a lack of knowledge of how to bring their work to market. Individuals who pursue this route should expect to receive minor royalties in return. Understand that the vanity publisher takes no risk whatsoever. In addition, the publishing company will be paid first, then, and *if* your book sells, they will take their cut and then pay you what is left over.

Four examples of vanity presses would be Author Solutions, Outskirts, Xulon Press (a publisher that focuses primarily on Christian titles), IUniverse, and there is a host of others. Keep in mind that a vanity press exposes you to abuse because there is little incentive to keep their costs down, or to do a good job.

Does this mean that a vanity press cannot do a good job? No. However, most professionals and Indies will tell you it is the least desirable route to be published. David Gaughran has quite a bit to say about the issue and you can check out his blog at the link here.

Traditional Publishing (They pay you)

Traditional publishers pay you for your work. More specifically, you are selling them the rights to print and distribute your work. They will provide you with professional editing, cover design, and some level of marketing. In addition, they might pay you an advance, which are initial upfront monies against which they expect the book to make: after those initial monies are recouped by the publisher, then the publisher will pay you a percentage of monies on future sales of your book. Remember, they will pay you these royalties from the sales of your books *after* the advance has been paid off. The industry standard is 10% for paperback and 25% for eBooks. Five major publishers dominate the publishing industry: Penguin Random House, HarperCollins, Hachette, Macmillan, and Simon & Schuster. They have many subsidiaries, and there are smaller publishing houses as well.

This method of publishing is the "popular" or traditional method that most authors in the past have typically aspired to attain. This method usually requires you to get an agent who, on your behalf, will solicit an editor within the publisher to read and gain the rights to print your work. Understand that with a publishing company, you and your work are an asset in a portfolio of other income-producing assets that comprises other authors and their work. Always understand your relationship to the person who is paying you, the money flow, and who has rights to your work. Traditional publishers primarily cater to book distributors, not to readers or authors. Again always, keep the relationships clear.

If you want to pursue this method, and desire to seek an agent to help you break into traditional publishing, peruse Google and search for publishing agents looking to take on new clients.

The following explains some of the various pros of traditional publishing.

Pros and Cons of Traditional Publishing

Pros of Traditional Publishing

Greater prestige

The reality is that traditional publishing is still considered sexier or having more prestige and or acceptance. It is also still the foremost way to see one's book on store bookshelves. However, being traditionally published is losing some of its status as indie authors are becoming increasingly adept at matching the quality of traditional publishers in content, marketing, and graphic design.

If you are an Indie author wanting greater prestige, I would suggest entering your book in writing contests and submitting your book to Publishers Weekly, and or Kirkus Reviews. Assuming your writing is good enough; these outlets will give you the positive strokes you need and affirm your writing chops by established leaders in the publishing community.

You can then leverage those bragging rights towards your promotional campaigns. This may also attract agents who are looking for new clients. The real question is, does cachet impact sales at all? This is where you must learn as an indie author how to use such accolades to your advantage.

Sizable advances

Even beginning authors can get good advances (if you have a good book proposal) Traditional publishers still are the best when it comes to earning *initial* income. Most other methods will not provide you thousands of dollars upon release of your book.

Seasoned editors

Traditional publishers have access to editors who can offer incredibly valuable creative and practical feedback. In addition, to more easily sell things like international and subsidiary rights to your book.

Professional, in-house designers to create great book covers.

These designers are aware of the latest trends and know how to put the best face forward on your work.

Active support of your marketing

While few publishers will do all your marketing for you, good ones will actively support your marketing efforts. A publisher will push your book if they determine that doing so will increase their profits. Traditional publishers will have access to marketing muscle that an indie author will typically not initially have.

Traditional Publishing 6 Cons

1. **It's slow**

It takes somewhere between 9-18 months for a book to be released once it is submitted to a traditional publisher, an infinity in the digital world we live in.

1. **It's unfair**

Traditional publishers take the lion's share of royalties, usually between 85-92%. That means most authors earn about a buck per book or less. Traditional publishers hog roughly 70% of electronic royalties, for a product that has almost no production or distribution costs.

1. **It's outdated**

They are not necessarily social-media savvy. Traditional publishers may have powerful in-roads to traditional media, like TV and print magazines, but those things are increasingly becoming irrelevant to book sales in the age of social media and digital marketing.

1. **It's ineffective**

They do not give most authors a big marketing push or sometimes any marketing push at all.

1. **It's short-lived**

Most authors' books will be in bookstores for a few weeks and then are pulled from the shelves when they do not sell very well, leaving it entirely up to Amazon sales. Of course this begs the question: why not just use Amazon?

1. **It's not cost-effective**

The vast majority of authors do not make any real bankable money on their books.

Independent publishing aka Self-publishing (you pay yourself)

Independent publishers are individuals who take it upon themselves to take ownership of the entire process of publishing. The author essentially does the graphic art, editing, marketing, layout, typesetting etc. herself or she contracts those services out. You choose your printer and distributors for your book, and you market your book. This form of publishing has skyrocketed because of Amazon and other book distributors' ease in both creating digital and print books, and selling those works directly to customers. This option will give you the most freedom in decision-making, allows the most income for the typical author, but also requires the most work in time and energy.

My journey to indie publishing

I t was sometime back in 2004 or 2005 when the idea for my novel came to me. I wanted to tell a story about what I believed was the epic tale of the fall of Lucifer. I had always been fascinated by the story of an angel who had betrayed God, and I had not seen as of that time anything that seriously tried to tell the story in a way that I thought was both serious and biblical. I decided in my audacity that I would try my hand at telling the story.

Seven years later, I finished my first draft after experiencing unemployment twice, divorce from a 23-year marriage and stepping down from ministry because of my divorce. In addition, I lost my job of three and half years and was making income at a far lower level than what I once had. In fact, I was so cash poor that at one point I left work knowing I did not have enough gas to get home and waited an hour before I hit the road so my direct-deposited check would clear my bank account, so that I could get enough gas at the corner gas station near my job so I could make the return trip home. Thus, amid a very trying time in my life, I completed the first draft of my novel on July 4th, 2013.

I had learned enough from reading books and various magazines that I knew I needed to obtain an agent, and so I tried on my own to submit my manuscript to a literary agency. They promptly let me know they were not enthusiastic enough about the project and wished me the best.

It was then that I decided I needed to be my own agent, that I had enough enthusiasm to do it and thus began my journey of indie-publication. Now prior to this, I had gained the monies to get graphic design work done for a cover and had another $500 for editing. I also had a couple of beta readers look at it, and one gave me some good developmental feedback. However, my social circle simply did not comprise people. I could give the book to help me edit it prior to its release. I reached out to a person who I thought would be a great person to both learn from and share. But the feedback I received was so negative and from a professed Christian no less that I ended up having to cut off association with the person, as it became mentally unhealthy for me. Eventually, this person would later come back to actually cyber-stalk me and write negative things about me on Amazon review page.

In November 2013, several months after I completed the first draft. I uploaded my book to Amazon's KDP and created a print version using what was then called CreateSpace.

I proceeded afterward to do several Internet radio interviews and used a blog tour to help spread the word. Reviews started pouring in. Overall, people enjoyed the read. I was very active in finding reviewers who might enjoy my type of fiction and spread the word. I created a blog using WordPress.com, and a Facebook author's page was eventually created besides my joining Twitter and Google Plus.

While all that was happening, I was getting reviews that showed how much I needed to have my work edited beyond what I had initially done. Please note that I had it edited. But enough comments came back from reviewers that I decided I needed to invest further in the book to make it the best product that I could. I eventually got a second edit from another editor, and my experience was much better than my first.

In addition, I wanted to make the book available to people in bookstores. Call it vanity, confidence, naivete, or whatever you desire, but I wanted to make sure anyone could go into the store and order a copy. So I gained a publisher's account through Lightning Source (aka Ingram Spark) and uploaded the book there.

Reviews came slowly, and I corrected various errors that I found later in the manuscript, and over time, made it better and better. I had to resubmit the print version of my book to Lightning Source several times, which caused me to shell out more cash for multiple revisions. It was a maddening process.

Now, during this time, I was still being trolled by my earlier acquaintance, who made it a point to negatively comment on any critical reviews that I received from readers. After 7 years, and after spending months getting the book edited, a brilliant cover made, and after spending over one thousand dollars in getting my book to meet some modicum of professional standards. I also spent about another $150.00 towards a blog tour. I earned at the end of Jan 2014 from my eBook sales, $11.44 from the sale of six books.

Yep, $11.44 cents. Yeah, really, eleven dollars and forty-four cents.

Would *you* be discouraged at this stage after investing over $1200.00 in a project to make back $11.44 cents? Would *you* be discouraged after realizing that you still needed to pour even more money into the project to make it better? What would you do if you had a person who had not even read your book, but was actively out to speak against it? What would *you* have done?

Now for some, all of the above might have been discouraging, but I received enough early reviews to know that I was onto something, and if I could expose my book to enough readers who believed in the value in what I had produced, I believed that the work would speak for itself.

I am happy to report that as of the date of this writing the book has done above all that I could have asked or thought, and while the novel is not, of course, for everyone's taste, (no book ever is.) 4 out of 5 people generally like the work.

Since that time, the book has picked up even more positive reviews, and my platform has dramatically improved, I even have the book in audio format now for readers, and it too has garnered positive reviews. Multiple books now have been written with more books on the way.

So let us look at my actual sales numbers. My total eBook sales in Jan 2014 were a whopping six books. For a total dollar amount of $11.44

Below is an actual screen capture of my actual eBook sales sold during the month of Jan 2015 for a total of $116.77

Actual sales for January 2015 were 66 in eBook sales from Amazon.

Below is a screenshot of my audible sales dashboard and Audible royalties for the month of Jan 2015, which was $598.63

Actual Audiobooks sold during Jan 2015

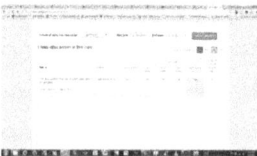

Total sales income for Jan 2015 was $715.40. This is one year later.

I want to emphasize that I am not an author who sells millions of copies. However, I sell enough to generate income every month from this first fictional book.

Now the reason that I gave the numbers is to show that I actually sell books. In addition, I am selling more all the time. Some authors sell more, some much less. If you are an author and you are selling only a few books a month, I believe my knowledge can help you.

I have become better at my business. I now understand how to become successful and I see the day coming where if I desired; I could write full time.

I expect once I show you the practical things you can do to position you for success; you can do the same or even better.

Currently, as of this writing, my monthly eBook sales are now past the five-hundred-dollar mark. Sales success is not about an instant event. It is about making progressive improvement in your sales over time with incremental steps. Most of us will not sell thousands of copies on our first outing. However, we can make continuous improvement to where we can make 100-200 sales a month.

Which option should I choose? My journey towards Indie publishing

So all of this ultimately leads back to asking the question; which publishing option should I choose? In order to determine which option best fits you; you must determine how much control over the publishing process you desire to have. How much are you willing to surrender in profits for your work? For example, if you have a lot of money to invest up front but are not willing to put in the time needed to contract out and monitor the different aspects of publishing, and you do not want, or are unable to go the traditional route, then vanity publishing is actually a realistic option for you.

Other questions you need to ask yourself; is where do you want to have your book distributed: on bookstore shelves, print, ePub, or audiobook? Are you satisfied with digital products only? The formats you want to see your book in will strongly influence which option you choose. If you just want to be online only, then indie publishing is your best route. Do you want to seek an agent? Are you willing to learn new skills or contract tasks out? Which format best assists you in reaching *your* readers? These are questions you need to ask yourself.

Once you take the time to answer these questions, again your options will better present themselves. I advocate beginning authors use the indie approach. It is economical, you can learn as you go, you are in control; you do not have to do every task yourself; you make the most profit, and you do not give up the option to go the traditional route if you would like to pursue this in the future. Because this is the approach I recommend, I will spend the rest of my time on how to bring your book to market and do so successfully via that approach. Since I recommend the indie-publishing route, let me attempt to dispel some myths associated with it before we delve deeper.

Independent-publishing has essentially five steps. To be successful in your authorpreneurship endeavors, you must excel in each of the five. It is that simple. Here are the steps.

1. Writing: You write the best story possible, most have this part down.

2. Editing: You polish your story to a shine by removing anything that detracts from the reading experience. You will do this following the three stages of editing (Well, talk about these later.)

3. Dress it up: People judge a book by its cover. It better be good, and your internal layout also needs to be up to par. This area includes what I call layout & cover design.

4. Publishing/Distribution (Who is going to publish it and distribute it?)

5. Registrations of your work (There are several registrations you will need depending on your publishing goals. ISBN's LCN's,)

6. In which format will you make your book available to the public? (eBooks, Print, Audio-book?)

7. Marketing (How will you find the audience who wants to read your work, and how will you promote to them?) This step happens to be the most difficult step for many authors; it's where the real business side of having to sell a product to the market comes into play.

Fundamentally, it does not matter if your book was published by Harper and Collins, or if you do it yourself. The same steps apply. What is fundamentally different about each publishing option is the degree of control you have over each step, how long each step takes, and the amount each of these steps might cost you in terms of your eventual profits. Now, if you feel there is an element that you are not adept at, take heart. YOU CAN LEARN TO IMPROVE AND GET BETTER!

What does it take to write your novel?

The actual act of writing your book comprises several steps. These steps assume a work of fiction.

Step 1: Gather the "star stuff" of inspiration. In other words, what images, sounds, research etc. anything inspires you to take the ideas that you have and put them to paper? What is the nucleus of your story that is clamoring to be written? Consider this step the primordial ooze of your novel.

Step 2: Gather your writing tools (dictionaries, grammar books, etc.)

Step 3: Develop your characters first (write their backgrounds, motivations, antagonists, story arcs, etc.)

Step 4: Develop your world (Kingdoms, laws, magic or no? What rules govern your world? etc.)

Step 5: Outlining (what is the meat of your story? What is the inciting incident that launches your story? What is your middle and the end?)

Step 6: Write! (Patience, persistence, and write fast to get the story out. When you write that first draft it is about progression towards completion, not perfection.

Step 7: Get some beta readers to review the best draft that you finish.

Step 8: Revise, Revise, and Revise again.

Step 9: Celebrate and put the book down.

Myths about indie publishing

MYTH BUSTED

Myth: It will be free or cost you nothing.

Fact: There are multiple costs that you will have to pay for.

While actually writing your work and uploading it to a distributor like Amazon is a no cost process in and of itself. In all likelihood, you will have to tackle the above costs in making your work look as professional as possible. And the figures listed are basement numbers! Most authors, while good in one area, will not typically be good in all the major aspects of publishing and still manage to not pay a dime. People who are telling you that self-publishing costs nothing are simply not telling you all the costs. Or have such a high skill level that they can indeed manage every single aspect of publishing without contracting out for help. Or last, they are simply displaying their ignorance about the costs.

Myth: You can do it totally with no external help

Fact: You will need to assemble a team to successfully create and promote your book.

A wonderful author by the name of Rochelle Carter in her book The 7 Step Guide to Authorpreneurship (Plan, Write, Publish!) has stated in her book,

"There is no such thing as self-publishing. Publishing is always a collective effort, and no single individual, no matter how immersed in the field, can complete it alone. Be it printing, shipping, converting to an eBook, marketing, distributing, editing, designing, or maintaining a visible and relevant social presence, somewhere along the publishing process, even the most determined and independently minded author will likely need some help publishing her book."

You will need help beyond your level of skills to be successful in your self-publishing efforts. If traditional publishers need a team of individuals to bring a book to market, expect that you too must also assemble one. This will happen by your contracting out or bartering services to others.

- **Myth: You will make lots of money!**

Fact: While it is possible to make lots of money. It will typically take time, and requires much investment in time and energy and yes, money on your part to see an adequate return on your initial investment. How quickly and how much is based in part of how much you contract out other services (editing, layout, graphic design, and marketing) that you yourself cannot do. But make no mistake, it will take time. In general, I advise authors to give it nine months before you see a return on your investment on a book.

- **Myth: Once you publish your book, you are done.**

Fact: The actual work begins now. Publishing your book on Amazon actually takes less than 15 minutes of your time. However, Amazon has literally millions of books. How then does one go about letting people know about the book? How do you drum up sales? How do you promote the book? These skills are lacking in many writers because they see themselves primarily as writers and not as business-persons or sales-persons that are bringing a product to market.

What does it cost to self-publish one's book?

I have seen blogs and Facebook posts that talk about how much it costs to publish. But the reality is that the cost of self-publishing one's novel will vary and depends a LOT on a person's skill level, network and their access to hardware and software that some of us simply take for granted.

Theoretically, self-publishing indeed can indeed cost you nothing. However, as we shall see, as we go further, your costs will vary, depending on what skills you have and where are you starting in the publishing process. I will repeat; it simply varies for most people

Writing the book in most cases should hopefully cost you nothing. You take some paper and pen and get to writing. Or if you are like me, you get on your PC and you peck away at the keys until you complete your manuscript.

But (and I've encountered this with a person.) what if you write your work on paper, but are not computer literate enough to use MS Word or other types of word processing programs to digitize your work? What if you have a completed a draft on paper but you can't type? What if you don't have access to your own PC?

Well, here will be the first hurdle or step for a writer like this: because you simply must digitize your work. The writer whose starting point begins here has several options. Either you must take the time and energy to do it yourself or you will have to find someone who can take your physical manuscript and type it into a word processor. There is actually a third option. You can buy speech to text conversion software and the ancillary hardware to "type" it out for you. (No clue on the total costs here.) If you need a person to help you type. You can look on Craigslist, Fiverr.com, www.writer.ly or elance.com to assist you. (This assumes, of course, the unavailability of a loved one or friend who can do it for you.)

How much would this cost? I would say anywhere from free to maybe a couple hundred dollars. Because if you are taking a physical written draft and giving it to someone to type it up for you (i.e. putting it into a word processor.) I can only assume you will want a copy of the document.

Assuming, however, you are not starting at such a basic level of having no computer access or the inability to type your own document, then writing the actual book should cost you nothing. In which case, so far so good!

It takes some money so use other peoples!

While publishing your book does not need to be expensive, it costs money. While you can search for cheap options in terms of design, and haggle down your editing costs, you will be lucky to get through the publishing process by spending less than $500. Oh, and remember that you get what you pay for.

I know for me I had the mindset that I wanted to become a professional who works with professionals. I loved my novel enough to pay for the best that I could afford.

If you are looking at a funding option, you might consider Kickstarter, which is the most popular crowd-funding option out there, which allows your fans to invest in your book. (This option works best, however, if you already have a following.) The best part is that you do not need to pay the money back. Instead, you offer rewards to people for backing your project (like pre-orders, posters, etc.). Other crowd-funding options include Indiegogo—launched in 2008, originally to fund independent films, Pubslush, RocketHub, and Unbound.

So do not let the challenge of insufficient funding stop you; barter what skills you have with others to help you get your work out there.

The process of creating your book.

E diting your book is about refinement. It is about taking away those things that are distractions for the reader, and making your prose as smooth as possible. While there are many books out there that can give you excellent advice on how to edit. My purpose in this book is simply to explain some simple steps. You can elaborate on them if you feel it is necessary, of course. But essentially, to get your work to a professional shine, you need to do at least these three steps before you release your book.

1. Acquire Beta Readers (This is your first step in editing)

2. Self-Revision (Do this after you have received feedback from your beta readers.)

3. Professional Editing: Determine what type of editing you will need.

What is a Beta Reader?

A beta reader (or beta reader, or beta) is a person who reads a work of fiction with a critical eye. The aim is to improve grammar, spelling, characterization, and smoothing the general style of a story prior to its release to the public. Another way to think of a beta reader is as a product development tester. Essentially, you have someone who represents a sample demographic of the market for your book to gauge consumer reaction.

I like the idea personally of a beta reader being more than someone who checks for grammar, spelling and the like. And thinking of this person(s) as representative of your selling demographic will really tell you if you are writing connects with your audience, and what you might need to do to improve.

Where can you find Beta Readers?

There are various areas that you can look for Beta-readers. A few of the best I'll just list out and link for you.

1. Family/Friends

2. LinkedIn (Look in various writing groups for people who will read your story

3. Goodreads.com

Join various groups on Goodreads; there are people in these groups who would love to read your story and give feedback.

1. Absolutewrite.com

2. Facebook

The reality is that there are many places you can find readers to help edit your story. Wattpad and Reddit are also great places to get feedback.

What are the basic steps?

1. Send out your manuscript.

2. Get back the replies.

3. Go through the replies, and thank each person by email, phone or a mailed note. A small gift is always appreciated as well!

4. Follow up and see if they will look at further work.

5. Determine if their input warrants change to your draft.

Things to watch out for

Now this might shock you, but you may very well have people who do not respond! Yep, you might have some that say they will beta read, and you provide them with the section they are to read, and they simply do not follow through for whatever reason. So you want more than just a couple of readers.

Second, be very clear on what you are expecting from a beta reader. Having a reader tell you the story was good, or that it was awful will not help you become a better writer. What was awful? Why? The more you can help focus your reader on monitoring how they are experiencing your work; the better off you will be.

Third, decide how much of your work you want to give out. Will it be a couple of pages, a scene, a chapter? The complete novel?

My recommendation is that you give out based on whether you trust the person to not steal your work, and are they are providing quality feedback? So start small, then give more to them as they show an interest and the ability to provide you with the quality feedback that you are looking for.

Questions to ask beta readers

Interest: Does the story hold your attention?

- Were you ever bored during the story?

- Was your mind ever wandering?

- Can you tell me in the story where it happened?

- Where do you remember losing interest?

World creation: is more detail needed?

- Was there ever an occasion during the story where it seemed not "believable"?

- Was there a point where you said, "Oh come on!"

- Were they any 'logical fallacies' that you noticed?

Exposition: How was it handled?

- Where in the story were you confused?

- Was there anything you had to read twice?

Characters

- Are there characters you found you did not care about?

- Did you like the character(s)?

- Did you hate the character(s)?

- Did you keep forgetting who the characters were?

Plotting

- Was there any plot questions left unresolved for you?

- Tension: Are the plot lines resolved?

- What do you think will happen next?

- What are you still wondering about?

Things to keep in mind

Remember that your reader is reporting on their experience of what they are reading, so their opinions are not wrong. They are helping you gain clues on how a reader is interfacing with your writing, and never forget to tell your readers thank you!

One great thing about your readers is that after they are done, you can use the information to help market your book. Beta readers can provide you with some great quotes or reviews to help speed you along your marketing way! Those quotes can also be used in promotions. Just make sure you have permission to quote them.

How to handle family beta reviewers

Remember that if there are concerns that a family member might not be objective, ask them to review it without revealing that it is your work. Let them know you are reviewing it yourself and trying to get some feedback from a different perspective. Because they are doing it for you, not only might they be inclined to do it but also you can get honest feedback without the prejudice since they do not know it is from you.

5 Self-Editing Tips

1. Edit to make sure the plot is sound first.

2. Edit for character development second (flesh them out as much as possible.).

3. Edit for word usage, grammar, and spelling third.

4. Get rid of Ly words (use your word processor's find feature to examine them.).

5. Use the "speak selected text" feature in MS Word.

Now editing can be hard. I know it is the most problematic part for me as a writer. The simple graphic below shows why it can be a challenge to self-edit one's own work.

Types of editing

Why it is hard for you to self-edit

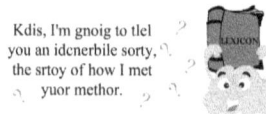

Kdis, I'm gnoig to tlel
you an idcnerbile sorty,
the srtoy of how I met
yuor methor.

You can probably read this. And the reason you can is that the mind automatically attempts to make sense of it. While this helps us to understand, it does not bode well for writers, and thus is one of the reasons you must have someone edit your work.

In my opinion, the two most important types of editing that an author needs are substantive editing and copyediting. Below are simple explanations of various types of editing which will help you understand what type of editing you need.

Substantive editing

Substantive editors work with you once you have a full text. These editors will help you get it into its final form. This may involve reordering or rewriting segments of it to improve readability, clarity, or accuracy. For a fiction writer, a substantive editor can alert you to inconsistent character behavior or speech, Help adjust your language to your desired audience, and make sure the story has believable dialogue and a plausible plot-line.

Copy editing

Copy editors work with your text when it is in final or nearly final form. They read each sentence carefully, seeking to fix all errors of spelling, punctuation, capitalization, grammar, and word usage, while preserving your meaning and voice. With your permission, they may rewrite tangled sentences or suggest alternative wordings. They can ensure that your text conforms to a certain style.

The Critique

The critique is generally a collaborative effort between the editor and the author and includes Reading for basic sense and coherence, consistency, dialog, pacing and descriptive passages. After reading, the editor will write an analysis of the strengths and weaknesses of your manuscript, with specific examples and suggestions on what you can do to improve it. The editor will return the hard copy containing notes throughout based on manuscript length.

The First Line Edit

A comprehensive sentence-by-sentence edit which includes reading through the entire manuscript, smoothing out awkwardly worded sentences, querying the author if something isn't clear, looking out for factual inconsistencies, query odd-sounding dialogue, and checking for anything that strikes the editor as "off."

Editing Resources

Below are web resources that I have found that will answer the bulk, if not all, of an author's editing questions. Below is a brief description of what you will find at each site.

1. *Common Editing Rates* (Will give you an idea of what is a reasonable rate to expect)
   http://www.the-efa.org/res/rates.php

2. *How to Find the Right Editor, Part 1: The Writer's Wish List Make sure you know what you want from an editor with the first part in this series.* http://www.righttoucheditin g.com/how-to-find-the-right-editor-part-1/

3. *How to Find the Right Editor, Part 2: Types of Editing - Learn more about the different kinds of editing and how they can work for you.* http://www.righttouchediting.com/h ow-to-find-the-right-editor-part-2/

4. *How to Find the Right Editor, Part 3: Testing an Editor - Before you dish out any money, make sure you are making a wise investment.* http://www.righttouchediting.com/ho w-to-find-the-right-editor-part-3/

5. *How to Find the Right Editor, Part 4: Finding Your Editor - So you know what editors you need, here is how to find them.*

Where to Find Editors

There are a variety of places where you can find competent editors. Below are just a few places to get you started on your journey to finding an outstanding editor for your publishing team.

The Five Steps of Indie Publishing

1. Author referrals: Always ask fellow authors whom they use. If the person is good enough for them, he/she might be good enough for you. Message the person on Facebook or contact them noting that you have been referred by an author they work with. Most editors are happy to discuss their work with you.

2. Freelance/Auction (Essentially, you auction the need for editing services or these links provide editors looking for work..

   a. http://www.paper-perfect-editing.com/

   b. http://www.the-efa.org/job/joblist.php

   c. https://www.odesk.com/

   d. https://www.crowdspring.com/post-a-project/

3. LinkedIn, Facebook, are also great places. Search through each social media's search

engine and groups to find the services you need.

As an Indie author, you will need to do the layout and design yourself or contract out those services. Layout Design encompasses both the interior and exterior of your book.

- Interior Design (includes but is not limited to).

  - How your book's content is arranged

  - Number of pages

  - Pagination

  - Illustrations

- Exterior Design (includes).

  - Front cover, side spine, and back cover

  - Back jacket narrative

  - Bar coding

Here are some places you can get great the covers made for your book.

Each has various price points, so depending on your budget, you can find excellent covers for your book.

- https://99designs.com/book-cover-design (My top recommendation.)

- http://www.selfpubbookcovers.com/index.php (Easily find covers under $100.00)

- http://authormarketingclub.com/members/pre-made-book-covers/

- http://www.designcrowd.com/?registrationmodal=true (Similar to 99designs.

Here are some tools you can use to do internal layout yourself

Download the software (it's free!) you will need software like this to convert your word document to the kindle MOBI format or into ePub format.

Scrivener (paid) is the superior option in my opinion and can convert it for you as well. Keep in mind that if you are going to use Amazon only, you can simply write your document in Microsoft Word, then upload it to Amazon and they will convert it for you. However, this is not necessarily the best method, but is doable.

Amazon KDP currently has another tool that will allow you to do your internal layout. It's called   While it does a wonderful job in laying out an excellent file; you will not be able to download a mobi copy of the actual copy of the file, which is a drawback to me. However, if this is not important to you, it's an excellent free solution.

If you are doing the internal layout yourself, make it a point to do what is called an active table of contents. An active table of contents is a table of contents in a digital book that, when you click it, it takes you the exact entry listed on the contents page. The YouTube link below will explain how to create an active table of contents in MS Word.

You can always pay someone to do these last two steps. is a great place to find someone to do this work for you.

Quick Internal Layout Tips (For print books)

1. Pagination: Always put odd #'s on the right page.

2. Even #'s go on the left page.

3. Your pages should be fully justified.

4. Don't put blank pages on the right side of your spread.

5. Blank left spread pages are ok.

6. No text on the page means no page #'s on the page.

7. No running head on the page means no page #'s on the page.

One resource that is also helpful is the LightningSource Cover Template Creator.

This is an excellent free resource you can use to make sure that if you are creating a print cover that the measurements are just right. Per Lightning Source, "*Once you complete and submit the form..., LSI will email you back a template and support files to be used to build your cover. Included in the email will be instructions for using the template, creating an appropriate PostScript file and distilling a PDF to LSI specifications.*" The link is listed below.

https://www.lightningsource.com/covergenerator.aspx

Now the wonderful thing about this is that you can use the files to create your cover for Amazon's Createspace as well. What works for Lightning Source I've discovered will work also for Createspace.

Book Layout Order

Listed below is the order of how content should be presented in your book if you plan to do the book's interior yourself.

- Title page: might include just the title and author; can include edition and publisher.

- Copyright page: publishing information, ISBN, CIP, copyright holder, year.

- Reviews: may or may not be included in a book; this is where you commonly would see them.

- Dedication

- Table of contents.

- Foreword

- Introduction

- Other front matter might include maps (such as in military planning), list of abbreviations, etc.

- Chapters

- Conclusion, Afterword, Epilogue.

- Appendixes: explanations and/or elaborations of chapter material.

- Chronology

- Endnotes

- Glossary

- Bibliography or references.

- List of contributors.

- Index

- If a book is a hardcover, it is common to have the author information on the cover wrap. Otherwise, if a book is a softcover, the author's information might be on the back cover or inside, after the conclusion.

Page Layout Software

In order to digitize your work, you need to use software to type up your manuscript. While there are many to select from; your hardware will in some way shape which software you use. I recommend the following pieces of software.

- Microsoft Word (the king of word processors, some find it too bulky to use for extensive works, however.

- Scrivener (my top recommendation designed specifically for the purposes of creating a book). Go to https://www.literatureandlatte.com/scrivener.php to get the software. You can check it out for free for a test run.

These recommendations are really all you need to write an eBook.

While formatting and layout for an eBook is rather simple. If you intend to create a print version of your book, there are certain types of software you will need to layout the pages properly.

- Adobe InDesign: The industry standard but expensive, with a high learning curve; if you are new or fearful of learning new software, then look elsewhere.

- Microsoft Publisher.

- Microsoft Word (again possible to do, but can be difficult in large documents.

Book Layout Designers

If you think you're not up to the task of laying out your book. Go to and type in 'Book layout'. Several inexpensive options will come up that you can use to assist you. Book formatting does not have to be expensive. Also, here is a link to where you can get free templates for your book layout.

Authors Streams of Income

Successful authors make money from turning their products into different formats. In other words, do not see your book as just one product, but several. It can be turned into Print, an eBook, an audiobook, a script, a comic, etc. Below are some of the ways to create a different format for the same book.

eBook (easiest type of book format to produce and to acquire immediate income)

Print (more expensive than an eBook to produce, usually takes more time to create, typically generates less revenue for the indie author but is more prestigious. However, harder to distribute to your readers.)

Audiobooks (lots of revenue potential, large market, requires much upfront investment in money or time.)

Boxed sets (great source of revenue once you have a series that you can sell as a volume set.)

Non-traditional distribution streams. (You can sell your books to specialty shops, airports, etc.)

Keep in mind that every time you see a book turned into a movie or television show, you are seeing this process at work.

Types of covers needed depending on your publishing goals

Your publishing goals are will determine what type of book cover you will need. For example, if you are just publishing for the eBook market, then you just need the front cover of your book, as shown below. This type of cover does not require a spine or back cover.

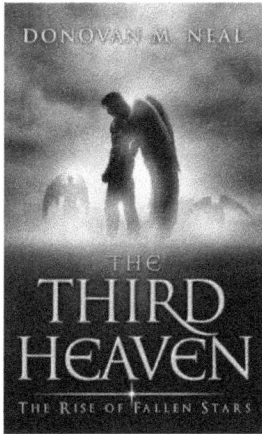

eBook cover

Marketing Basics

Print book covers requires both a spine and back cover.

Also, print books will need a bar code that goes on the back of the book. You can get this code generated for you for free if you use the Lightning Source cover template creator that I recommended earlier.

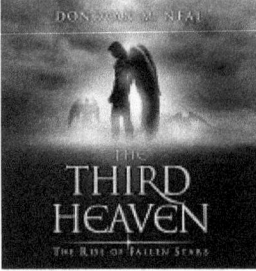

Audiobook covers are like eBook covers in that they do not need a spine or back jacket. However, their dimensions are different. Know what types of cover you are required to produce for the format of your book. Amazon's audiobook publishing arm ACX requires that all of their covers be square. Cover dimensions need to be no smaller than 2400 X 2400 pixels in size but less than 8 MB. Images must be 24 bit, no smaller than 72dpi, and must be RGB (not CMYK). Again, the images must be squared. The squared cover must be a true squared cover and cannot be rectangular with colored borders on the side. (CD case cover/jacket, e.g.)

Copyright, ISBN's and Library Control Numbers

Depending on what your publishing aspirations are, decide about acquiring an ISBN and an LLCN. If you want your book in bookstores, then you will need to get an ISBN from Bowker.

Although you can get a free one from Amazon, you need to understand this will make Amazon the publisher of record of the book, and bookstores are typically not interested in helping Amazon make money, which means that book buyers at bookstores will be less inclined to purchase your book for their floor. Note that an ISBN is a requirement for print book distribution. For eBooks (especially on Amazon's distribution platform), they are unnecessary. My recommendation is that you spend the money to acquire the ISBN for you book if you really want to see it in bookstores.

Library Congress Control Number

An LLCN is only required if you plan to have your book in libraries. In which case you will need to register with https://www.loc.gov/programs/preassigned-control-number/about-this-program/and you must be your own publishing company to do this.

Copyright Registration:

Yes, you want to register your books as copyrighted. A common misconception is that once you have written something that it is not already copyrighted, this is incorrect. Per the copyright office website: "Your work is under copyright protection the moment it is created and fixed in a tangible form that it is perceptible either directly or with the aid of a machine or device."

Therefore, as an author, what you are really seeking is to have your work registered as copyrighted. Here are two questions people typically have about registering a copyright.

Do I have to register with the copyright office to be protected?

No, registration is voluntary. Copyright exists from the moment the work is created. Register, however, if you wish to sue for infringement of a U.S. work

Why should I register my work if copyright protection is automatic?

Registration is recommended for several reasons. Many choose to register their works because they wish to have the facts of their copyright on the public record and have a certificate of registration. Registered works may be eligible for statutory damages and attorney's fees in successful litigation. Finally, if registration occurs within 5 years of publication, it is prima facie evidence in a court of law. See Circular 1, Copyright Basics, section "Copyright Registration" and Circular 38b, Highlights of Copyright Amendments Contained in the Uruguay Round Agreements Act (URAA), on non-U.S. works. So get your works registered!

Distribution and Product Placement

amazon kdp

kindle | direct publishing

draft 2 DIGITAL

N ow that your work is registered, properly edited, and jazzed up with a spiffy cover. Make some decisions on how you want to distribute your book or "product place" your book. There are several distribution options available to you as an indie author. In review, remember that your publishing model comprises vanity, traditional, indie, and hybrid. Assuming again that we are using the indie model, we need to ask ourselves what is the best way to distribute our shiny new product to our target demographic so that they can find it.

The traditional book distribution landscape comprises brick-and-mortar bookstores, e-retailers like Amazon, libraries, audiobooks, foreign language translations, and overseas sales. Let's tackle the most typical way of publishing for your book, which is an eBook through an e-retailer.

Indie authors focusing on their e-retail distribution really have only one choice to make: to publish beyond Amazon's ecosystem or not. Amazon has roughly 70% of the eBook market. So not doing business with Amazon is typically suicide for a beginning indie author.

If you want to stay within Amazon's ecosystem, then your choice is very simple. You enroll your eBook in Amazon's Kindle Direct Select Publishing Program, upload your book and you are off to the races. (Note there is a difference between KDP and KDP Select)

However, if you want to publish beyond Amazon, such as on Barnes and Nobles, iTunes, Scribed, Kobo, Overdrive, etc. Then you will need to go outside Amazon to do so. (Amazon will not help you get your eBook into these other smaller markets.)

What if I want to publish beyond Amazon?

If you choose to publish outside Amazon, you have another decision to make.

1. To publish with each individual distributor. (Barnes and Nobles, iTunes, Scribed, Kobo, Overdrive, etc.)

2. Or use an aggregator to distribute your book to various retailers. (Draft2Digital, IngramSpark).

You can publish directly to Barnes and Noble, iTunes (if you have a Mac computer) Scribed, and Kobo, and Overdrive, by simply following their upload guidelines. However, this requires you to track your manuscript for each individual distributor of your work. This might not be an issue if you only have one book, but can be very time-consuming if you have multiple books or a series.

However, placing your book directly also gives you more control over the categories that your book is placed in with the distributor, which has a direct impact on your discoverability, which directly affects your sales.

As mentioned, the second option involves using an aggregator, Draft2Digital, IngramSpark, and Bookbaby are currently the top three that currently dominate the market, with Draft2Digital being probably the most popular of the bunch.

Essentially, you upload your book once to the aggregator and then they will distribute your book to the other distributors. They will track your sales from each one and will pay you. All take a percentage of your royalties to provide the service; typically, this will be 15% of your royalties.

Let it be known that no matter if you upload directly to a distributor or you use an aggregator, you should ALWAYS upload directly to Amazon, as the lion's share of your sales will come from them.

Since I want this to be a small book that covers how to do things, and there is so much preference on what you as an author might want to do. I will not give a recommendation of which aggregator to use other than work through what issues are important to you. David Gaughran offers a great overview of these issues on his blog. You can look up his link that covers some of these here. https://davidgaughran.com/blog/

If you are an indie publisher, you have several good options that you can choose to print and distribute print versions of your book. There are my four recommendations.

1. Kindle Direct Publishing (KDP)

KDP or kindle directed publishing is Amazon's print on demand arm. This role was formerly had by CreateSpace, which was taken over by KDP. They can produce print quality books for you. Their set up is very easy, and it is free to set up your book. They will produce the least expensive book. However, they do not do hardcover books. Overall, their quality is good. They also offer an extended distribution option to get your book placed in bookstores. However, keep in mind most brick-and-mortar stores do not want to buy a book where Amazon is listed as the publisher. It would be like General Motors having to buy a Ford product. They are not trying to help their competitor. So, while you can indeed use Amazon as your publisher via the use of their free ISBN's I would recommend going through LightningSource or Ingram Spark using your own ISBN's if you want your book in brick-and-mortar stores. I use KDP to print books for trainings, author signings, and giveaways, as it is usually less expensive, and I use LightningSource for brick and mortar sales to avoid the stigma book buyers have with an Amazon published book, and to more closely conform to the book buying industry culture.

1. Lulu.com

Lulu.com is also a print distributor. Set up is easy and is free. A little more expensive to print your books, but not cost prohibitive. They do hardcover books. Print quality is about equal to KDP, in my opinion.

2. LightningSource/ IngramSpark

Lightning Source or Ingram Spark is the route you want to go if you desire to see your book in bookstores. However, be warned that their set up procedures can be challenging as they are set up to accommodate traditional publishing houses and not indie authors. In addition, set up can run $80.00. However, their quality is superior, and you will pay the most for printing through them. Again, if you want your books in stores, this is the way to go, in my opinion. Note IngramSpark is their indie author division and is the route I suggest you go. Lightning Source is typically not needed for the average author these days.

3. Draft2digital

Draft2digital is also an aggregator but has become extremely popular. You can create both eBook and print versions of your books. This is also a great way to place your books in stores apart from Amazon. Their process is straightforward and definitely should be given a look to see if you want to pursue publication of your work.

Audio Book publishers and distributors

If you want to produce an audio book, Amazon again leads the charge. ACX.com is the premiere means that allows you to take your work and put it in audio format. The process is straightforward. To get started, one simply needs to go to ACX.com and register. It is very simple, and as a person who has completed the process of having the audio version of his novels done, I can testify that it is as easy as they say.

How easy it is really depends on how much work you yourself want to do in narrating your own work.

Method 1

If you want to do it yourself; you simply record your narration, upload it to ACX, and create a cover

Once you have uploaded your narration and cover, ACX will distribute your work via Audible and iTunes.

If you have done your work and uploaded files to Amazon's KDP, then this process will be very familiar to you. The above is for authors who have the willingness to take matters into their own hands and do all the work in creating the audio product. I would also suggest that you have some voice acting talent if you have a fiction based product.

Method 2

If you are a bit too busy or do not feel you can do the narration justice; then you can enter a contractual relationship where you can split the proceeds with a voice actor. This method is called royalty share. Using this method, you will list your audiobook and solicit voice actors to audition for your work.

You will go through a menu process of selecting the type of voice. It is a very intricate process that forces you to think about what type of sound that you want from your narrator. Everything from the genre, gender, age, accent to vocal styles such as "authoritative" is available to choose from. The selection process will really make you think about how the story should sound.

Once you establish what type of voice you want. There are hosts of voice actors you can solicit to do your narration. Alternatively, you can request an audition by uploading a portion of your work, and having various ones read it. In my own situation, I had at least four auditions before I settled on my voice actor. Now, what is also fantastic is that Amazon has a program that will provide a stipend for the voice actor. I.e., Amazon will pony up the money up front for your work to be established, meaning you have no out-of-pocket cost. However, your book must meet certain criteria, but you can learn about the stipend program here.

Once you select your actor, there is an agreement that Amazon brokers between you and the actor where you split the royalties. Production begins after the contract is agreed upon.

Method 3

This method is the most expensive; you simply choose a narrator and pay them up front to produce the audiobook for you. However, let me offer a word of advice. You are entering a contractual arrangement when you agree with a narrator. Make sure you do due diligence before working with them and treat them as the professionals they are. Many authors fail to recognize that their narrator is a crucial piece of their audiobooks' success. Moreover, if you have a series of books; budget for the series for the one voice actor. Your buyers typically will not want you to change voice actors from book to book.

Marketing is one of the most important tasks the authorpreneur can undertake in order to be successful. Let me make this perfectly clear just in case you think you do not need or desire to market. Writing a novel without wanting to market it is like having a child without wanting to raise it. NO child without support and nurture could ever hope to survive or thrive. Likewise, your novel will flounder in the abyssal trenches of obscurity. Why wouldn't you do everything you can to make sure your book is a success? It's YOUR baby!

Since the original version of this book came out ACX now offers AI generated voices for your titles for free. But I noticed they appear to segregate these titles from their main catalog. So just something to be aware of.

Discoverability vs Sales

To successfully bring your book to the market, not only must you understand whom your audience is, you must also understand the crucial difference between discoverability and sales, and you cannot make sales if no one knows about your book. You could literally give your book away, but if you do not promote that giveaway, no one will know. Hence, the challenge for authors today is not how to get published–it is how to get noticed. Which begs the question, how do you get discovered?

To get discovered requires that you identify who your readers are, where they hang out, and how to connect with them. Therefore, you must devise a basic marketing plan that answers the following questions.

Who can you spread the word to?

What does your reader get from your product?

Where can you find people who also want your product?

When do your promote it?

How to identify your readers in 6 easy steps

Every author needs readers. Let us face it, without readers, no one will read your work. However, for many indie authors, especially those in small genres, it can be a challenge to find them. So how do you do it?

Here are several quick tips to find and build personal relationships with your audience. To find out where your readers congregate, I suggest you get on Goodreads.

Create author profiles on this site. Remember, you must be active in finding readers. Do not just think you can write a book, publish it, and your readers will find you. Go to them! You must be active in finding them.

Goodreads will have readers that will enjoy your book. I always tell people that there is a market for who you are. Goodreads contains the largest gathering of people who enjoy books.

So, Goodreads is a great place to begin your search. Sometimes people ask me about Facebook. While you can meet your readers in a group on Facebook, Goodreads has specific tools that we will use to help us gather information about our reader. Facebook is something we can use later when we find our reader and a relationship is established. Until then, I would not recommend it as a place to find your reader, but a place to interact with them once found.

Find the book that most resembles your work. This is a key step. What you are really doing here is assessing who your competition is in the marketplace. If you own an Apple iPhone, Samsung is going to be the phone that is most like yours. If you have written a fantasy book, then other fantasy books (especially those like yours) is what you want to actively find.

It is important that you have a good idea of which books bests resemble your work. For example, people who enjoy Star Trek might similarly enjoy Star Wars. So, understanding where in the literary world your book fits is extremely important. Amazon can also help you with this. If your book is published on Amazon, you can see which books Amazon's algorithms think are like yours, and or which books also fit into the category you have placed your book in. What you want to do is find the top ten books that are in your category and write those titles. Especially find those titles that are as close to your subject matter as possible. Keep that list handy.

Ask yourself the following questions to narrow down even more until we find that specific reader who would enjoy your book.

Genre– This is the easiest one, but do not be too general. You need to look at the subcategories of the genre. You cannot simply say your novel is a romance and be done with it. It is important to know the sub-genre, as not every reader reads every sub-genre of romance. Type in your book title on Amazon and see what titles are like yours. Readers who like your genre will probably like your work. Use Authors Marketing Central reviewer grabber to grab emails of the reviews of similar books.

Setting–If your story takes place in a real, recognizable place, the regional color you add can get the book into local bookstores and gift shops.

Theme–Think about who might resonate with the life lesson your novel teaches. If you are writing about single motherhood, you might find mom-bloggers with similar interests to be your ally.

Problem–If you are dealing with a real problem–autism, cancer, alcoholism, you might connect with readers facing those same issues.

Character–Your protagonist might represent your target market. Are they a surfer, a college student or a cat lover? Your character may belong to a professional, social, or ethnic group that will appeal to your reader.

You, the Author–if you bring certain knowledge to your book (say as an attorney or doctor writing a legal or medical thriller); you might look at your own affiliations for marketing ideas. (Look at people on social media who are like you. Check out persons on Twitter, Facebook groups, Goodreads, for persons who are like you in terms of interests.)

Keywords and their importance.

Amazon allows you to use keywords, which are words and or phrases that you or others might use to search for and or describe your book. Keywords (which can also be phrases) are important because they can place your book in additional categories on Amazon, giving you greater visibility among more readers. Amazon does not give you many methods to increase your visibility on their website. However, by changing your keywords in KDP, you can increase your visibility by having your book placed in additional categories beyond the two that Amazon automatically gives you.

The link below gives an excellent tutorial on how to maximize your keywords.

http://www.selfpublishingreview.com/2015/02/how-to-choose-kindle-keywords/

We have discussed how to get your book in brick-and-mortar stores, e-retailers and how to do an audiobook. However, if you want to expand even more into the area of traditional distribution, then you need to look at getting your book into libraries, having it translated into other languages, and increasing its distribution beyond your home country.

As an indie author, you want to make sure that your print book has an LLCN number. Libraries use the Library of Congress database, as well as other databases, to stay up-to-date on titles. It makes it easier for them to purchase your book by registering. Getting the number just helps libraries to discover you so they can order your book and it also conforms to their system of doing business. To get your eBook into their system is another matter altogether. Essentially, you can upload your eBooks directly to either of these distributors (Scribd, Overdrive, Odilo) or again use an aggregator like Smashwords. Keep in mind that you cannot be enrolled in Amazon's KDP Select program and distribute to other retailers, as KDP Select limits your ability to digitally distribute your work to Amazon only.

Foreign language translations comprise hiring a translator, then using the same principles to determine your market overseas. You can try Bablecube.com or contract with a translator on Elance.com as a possible method to get your book translated.

Non-traditional publishing options include but are not limited to specialty shops, prisons, airports, mass merchandisers, etc. Because there is so much in this area, I have included a few links to some more helpful information in the back of the book. However, because I want to keep this book short, and because this circle is in my mind for advanced authors: I am going to simply refer you to the best resource I have seen on the subject and that is How to Make Real Money Selling Books by Brian Jud. It covers in much more depth than what I can accomplish here. Proceed to this area after you have mastered some of the other ARC circles.

Understanding platforms and how to use them.

"Platform is the means by which you connect with your existing and potential fans." Michael Hyatt.

I absolutely love this definition; a platform is a merely a tool or a means to an end. It is a tactic, not a strategy. This lets us know that our platform then should be flexible to accomplish the goals we have created: i.e. to connect with existing and potential fans.

A solid platform has three characteristics:

1. Visibility to potential customers/fans.

2. It amplifies or extends your message.

3. It allows you to connect with people and engage them.

Based on the above, a blog can be a platform, a website, a Facebook page, Twitter, an email list, speaking engagements, etc. All these tools have the means to accomplish connecting with current and potential fans. Which tool is best will depend on your preferences and the work you desire to put into maximizing its effectiveness.

Imagine a house or a building. Keep in mind that the strongest structures are built on a solid foundation, and then as the superstructure is created, additional things can be put in, and atop it, like plumbing, electricity, etc. What, then, is the foundation that you should build your platform on?

I believe an email list is something that every author should strive for. An email list is your best means to contact your fans and influencers. It cannot be taken from you. It will not vary like Facebook rules. You own it, unlike other areas of "real estate" on the web. Real estate is a great way to think of platform. If you remember the game Monopoly, the ability to win at the game is subject to owning various pieces of real estate and then developing said real estate. As people passed the properties you owned, they gave you money. In the end, you won because you owned real-estate and invested the monies back into the purchasing of other investments (rail roads, water works etc.) to create a monopoly. Based on the cash you had, you were aware of what pieces cost the most money to develop and what other properties to shoot for. Thus eventually creating the monopoly needed to win the game.

Likewise, building a platform is like playing monopoly. Some pieces cost more than others did. (I.e. a self-hosted website) Some take more time to develop.

So here are some practical tips you can take to develop your platform:

Start a blog or website as a central place where you can be found online.

Create an email list (one of the most important things you can do!)

Engage in Social Media (Facebook, Instagram, Twitter, LinkedIn, Pinterest, Goodreads)

Develop a marketing plan of action

Ideally, all these things should be done before you even write your book!

Do the simple things to lay the foundation for your platform.

Make sure you have both a Goodreads and Amazon author pages

Make sure your priority is to get reviews (20 is a good initial number)

Make sure all versions of any book you have are available in both print and digital.

Always have the back matter of your book. Have a call to action that points to the next book or to your email subscribers list or some funnel to keep them connected with you.

How to create your author email list. (One sure-fire method!)

Sign up for an email newsletter service (Adwebber or Mailchimp, or MailerLite) I used Mailchimp to start. This will be the place where you collect your emails so you can create newsletters to send out to your email list.

Second, become friends with people on Goodreads. Seek people out who have similar interests, whom you can help support, and who might like you and or review your work.

Third, make sure that when you send out friend requests, get permission to give them something by becoming your friend.

Now here is the awesome part. When someone adds you as a friend on Goodreads, the friend's request usually will include their email address! Simply add those new Goodreads friends' emails to your email list! Viola, you are building your list with people who are engaged with you!

Wait! What about social media?

Social media is used to make connections with people. Do not use it to primarily try to sell your book. It can do that, of course. Success varies with the author.

5 uses of social media as an author

1. **Building the Brand** – by being useful, telling stories, answering questions, giving glimpses behind the scenes.

2. **Building Community and Engagement** – ask and answer questions, listen to feedback, support the goals of those you connect with.

3. **Building Trust and Credibility** – by showing you know what you are talking about and an understanding of the niche you operate in.

4. **Driving Traffic** – sharing links to new content and highlighting the best bits in your website archives.

5. **Building a presence in places that work best for you!** Twitter, Pinterest, Facebook, Instagram, LinkedIn etc. (Create relationships with and positive impressions upon those you connect with.

Remember!

Darren Rowse is the best blogger in the world. Yet his blog only brought in 7% of his eBook sales!

Promotion and Advertisement

Publicity, specifically promotion and advertisement, is the mechanism that will place your book before audiences. It is the lifeblood that pumps through a business. Without promotion and advertisement, you will forever languish in the quicksand of obscurity. Now, without getting fancy, I define promotion as simply *non-paid publicity that others generate about you and your product.* Using this definition, all forms of publicity are not the same, and this is important because this can help you understand and track how your publicity efforts are doing.

The most powerful form of publicity/promotion is word of mouth. Now we will look extensively about how to generate word-of-mouth promotion about your book that produces positive social proof about your book and contributes to sales.

There are several forms of promotion (i.e., non-paid publicity that you can avail yourself to.

Blogs (Find bloggers on the internet who will review your book for free.)

Free press releases (You can write out a press release and distribute it yourself to your local media.)

Internet Radio (There are thousands of podcasters out there who are looking for content to talk about. Go to Blogtalkradio.com and find producers who would be interested in talking about your book, or its subject matter.)

Social Media Promotion (Tweet your book, and post it on Facebook, and other social media.)

Product Reviews (straightforward, solicit readers on Goodreads, and Reviewers on Amazon to review your book. You give them a book in exchange for an honest review. You can go to Author Marketing Club.com and sign up for their premium membership to find reviewers, and get email addresses to reviewers who are interested in your book. Radioguestlist.com is another source to find producers to interview you.)

KDP Select (Amazon's own program has a promotional aspect that can generate free buzz about your book using timed sales, or free giveaways.)

Overdrive/via Smashwords: If you distribute your book via Overdrive you can use their program to distribute to Overdrive, which will make the book available to Libraries for free for digital download, increasing your discoverability.

Giveaways (Using a Goodreads giveaway to give away a print version of your book will put the giveaway before readers. People will see it and not just enter to win, but indicate it as a "to read" on their lists of books to buy. Also, do a LibraryThings.com giveaway to help spread the word.)

Advertisements

Now that we have looked at some promotional non-paid publicity options that you can use to get started, let us talk about advertisements. Ads are paid publicity that others generate about you and your product. You pay someone to promote you. Now when it comes to books, paid advertisement can do wonders to move your book before readers, increase discoverability and visibility and yes generate sales. The best way to get an advertisement for your book is to use a company that has its own list of readers that circulates books too. The biggest provider of such a list and the 800-pound gorilla in this regard is Bookbub. With millions of readers, this paid email circular will produce for you. In the next few pages, I will cover how to use each major type of paid advertisement and how to maximize your efforts using KDP Selects program on Amazon. Besides Bookbub, you must consider Amazon and Facebook as the top three platforms to pay for eyes on your books. Now this book will simply become too large if I tried to explain all the ways to maximize these three ad platforms. I cannot emphasize this enough. To be successful, you must advertise on Amazon or Facebook. Thankfully, there are excellent resources that will give you an in-depth and excellent understanding of how and why to advertise. In no particular order, I recommend the following must have resources to give you a complete understanding of the advertisement arena. Note: Since the original version of this book, Tik Tok has emerged as a colossus. Smart authors would investigate this latest platform as a means to expand discoverability and increase sales.

Distribution Options and Printers

1. Mark Dawson's Ads for Authors (an actual online class) Costly but worth it.

2. Help My Facebook Ads suck by Michael Cooper.

3. Ads for Authors who hate math by Chris Fox.

4. Strangers to Superfans by David Gaughran.

5. Bookbub Ads Expert by David Gaughran.

6. Mastering Amazon Ads by Brian Meeks.

What's a platform and why you need one?

Top 10 websites trafficked on the Internet as of July 2025

Rank Website Category Description

1 Google.com Search Engine The world's leading search engine and web portal.

2 YouTube.com Video Sharing The largest platform for video streaming and sharing.

3 Facebook.com Social Media The most popular social network globally.

4 X.com (formerly Twitter) Social Media Widely used for real-time news and social updates.

5 Instagram.com Social Media Major platform for sharing photos and short videos.

6 Baidu.com Search Engine China's dominant search engine.

7 TikTok.com Social Media Leading platform for short-form mobile videos.

8 Wikipedia.org Reference/Education The largest free online encyclopedia.

9 WhatsApp.com Messaging/Social Widely used messaging and communication platform.

10 Amazon.com E-commerce The largest global online retailer and marketplace.

The above listing is important because it helps to identify where your prospective buyers are hanging out on the web. Always check the rankings as they change consistently.

The below are paid book advertisers by U.S. traffic rank. Note: Kindle Nation Daily is a viable ad option but is not included in my count of the top ten, as they do not have a targeted email list to present your book to. I have not used their services to judge their effectiveness yet, but will report when I do. As of the update of this book, I also advise to find paid book advertisers who specialize in your genre: Bookbarbarian is a good example of this which specializes in fantasy and sci-fi.

Bookbub https://www.bookbub.com/partners/pricing

Ereadernewstoday http://www.ereadernewstoday.com/ (I've used)

Kindle Nation Daily http://indie.kindlenationdaily.com/ (does not have an email list option but can take an ad on their website.)

Bookgorilla.com http://www.bookgorilla.com/

Booksends.com formerly aka Bookblast http://booksends.com/advertise.php (I've used)

Fussy Librarian http://www.thefussylibrarian.com/submit/ (I've personally used)

Ebooklister http://www.ebooklister.net/

Ebooksoda http://www.ebooksoda.com/

Ebookblaster http://www.ebookbooster.com/

Outside the U.S. and misc.

http://www.freado.com/ rank 7,823 traffic rank in India

http://www.kboards.com/ads/

http://www.shewrites.com/

A new way to do book promotion via cell phones

http://www.genrepulse.com/how-it-works/

Great Publicity Options for authors

1. Email advertisements (Bookbub, Ereadernewstoday, FussyLibrarian. etc.)

2. Goodread giveaways (Giveaway print copies of your book for free to drum up discoverability)

3. Critical Book Review Sources (Kirkus Reviews, Net Galley)

4. Blog Tours (type in blog tour promoters in Google search, find one that works for you, http://www.thebookdesigner.com/2014/02/greg-strandberg/

5. Press Releases (Learn how to write a press release then pay for its distribution.

6. Awards (Search out book award competitions you can enter)

7. Blog Reviews

8. LibraryThing giveaway.

Author Marketing and your budget

U se this beginning strategy to get a lay of how you can spend your marketing dollars to increase discoverability and sales to your work.

Promotion Exercise: 1 (To be used with the "great publicity options for author's list above.)

The information below gives you an exact strategy to use based on the dollars you have available to market your book.

1. Determine how much you have available to spend on advertisements.

2. Then use any single or combination of the services listed in that price range to get the best value for your dollar.

3. Keep using the methods that work for you until you have enough of a budget to move into the next higher level.

<$50 Run a KDP select free promo or discounted promotion > any free email list advertisement) > Social Media promotion of your choice > Goodreads giveaways > Request Book Reviews from Bloggers >Internet Radio Podcasts > Do a LibraryThing giveaway > Run Amazon and or Facebook Ads (Most of these methods will generate the reviews you need, and help prime the pump for sales after the free period wears off. Best results are had when more than one book in a series exists, or where you have multiple titles.

$50> Ereadernewstoday > Bookgorilla > Booksends > FussyLibrarian or other preferred email list marketers of your choice. > Pay attention to which genre caters to you. > Run Amazon and or Facebook Ads (Also, do the lower level items)

$100> Blog Tour > Ereadernewstoday > Bookgorilla > Booksends > FussyLibrarian other preferred email list marketers of your choice. Pay attention to which genre caters to you. > Run Amazon and or Facebook Ads (Also, do the lower level items)

$500> Blog tour > Bookbub > Paid Press Release > Submit to Awards > Run Amazon and or Facebook Ads (Also do the lower level items)

$1000> Blog tour > Bookbub > Kirkus Review > Net Galley > Paid Press Release > Awards > Run Amazon and or Facebook Ads (Also do the lower level items)

$2000> Blog tour > Bookbub > Kirkus Review > Net Galley > Paid Press Release > Targeted Magazine Ads > Awards > Run Amazon and or Facebook Ads (Also do the lower level items)

$5000> Blog tour > Bookbub > Kirkus Review > Net Galley > Press Release > Targeted Magazine Ads > Awards > Run Amazon and or Facebook Ads (Also do the lower level items)

*See social media promotion exercise 2 to determine how to best use social media.

If you can afford it. Always run Amazon Marketing Service Ads. Brain Meeks has an excellent book on how to run ads on Amazon.

Promotion Exercise 2: How to run an Amazon KDP free giveaway campaign

1. Always run a KDP promotion over several days. My recommendation is for 3-5 days.

2. Let's say you're running a 3-day promo. On day 1 your KDP promo starts and, of course, runs through day 2 and 3.

3. Have one ad start on day 2, the 2nd ad on day three, etc. All the way through the end of the promotion. You want each ad to start on a different day of the promotion. One at the beginning, one in the middle, and one towards the end. This will help your sales go beyond just the time frame of the promotion itself.

Check out a promotion that I did and notice how I used two email list ads and staggered when each started. Each ad was laid on top of the running KDP promotion.

NEVER START ALL YOUR FREE CAMPAIGN ADS ON THE SAME DAY!!

Using the ARC, let us look at the seven aspects of your publishing business.

Author Marketing Cheat Sheet: PPC Ads vs. In-Person Events

Author Marketing Cheat Sheet: PPC Ads vs. In-Person Events

U se this guide to understand how online ad metrics translate to real-world book events. The principles are the same—you're just changing platforms.

Think of PPC Advertising Terms in light of what they mean at an in-person event.

Impressions = People walking by your table aka Foot traffic—how many people could potentially see you.

Clicks = People who stop at your table and check out your book Real interest—someone actually engages with you.

CTR (Click-Through Rate) = People who stop ÷ People who walked by, This measures how effective your table is at pulling people in.

Orders/Sales = Book purchases at your table The number of confirmed buyers.

ACOS (Ad Cost of Sale) = Table cost ÷ Total sales How much of your revenue is used to cover event costs. The lower the number = more efficient.

Applying ACOS to Author Events

- **Example:** If your table costs $100 and your goal is to maintain a 24% ACOS...

  - You need **at least $417 in book sales** to break even at that efficiency.

- ($100 ÷ 0.24 = $416.67)

- **Personal Rule of Thumb:**

  - *"I expect to sell 1 book per hour."*

  - This is your *performance benchmark*—a personal ACOS standard for in-person events.

  - Use it to decide if an event is worth attending from a profit standpoint. (*Is the juice worth the squeeze?*).

Why This Matters

Marketing isn't just about impressions or traffic—it's about **conversion and cost efficiency**. Whether you're running ads or attending events, you're playing the same game:
"How much am I spending to make a sale?"

Then track, adjust and repeat.

The below is the guideline I use when it comes to Amazon Ads. Adjust these guidelines to your taste to find that combination that works for you.

Donovan Amazon Ad strategy

1. Your book must support your ad costs.

a. Start with your print book; it gives you more wiggle room to make a mistake and recover

b. Start with the first in the series/if you have no first in series, start with the print version of your book.

c. After you've made a profit on your print book for 60-90 days, then run ads for the e-book.

d. No 99-cent cost books. The book must have a sales price of 3.99 or higher.

2. Target similar products (Find the ASIN's then grab 25 of them to run ads against. Find your Amazon Also-boughts or top 50 in genre as well.

3. Target appropriate keywords (grab 100 total)

a. Titles

b. Subjects

c. Themes

4. Target similar authors (grab 25 of them tops and run adds against those names)

5. Start with a $5/day budget of .34 cents with a lower bid.

6. What books in my catalog should I run ads for? (NOT ALL OF THEM!)

1. All stand-alone physical print titles that are $3.99 and higher that you want to increase their discovery.

2. Any first in series e-books that are priced at $3.99 and higher that you want to increase their discovery.

3. All box sets that you want to increase discovery.

Do not run adds of books 2 and 3 of series. Take people to the first book.

It is easier to run ads if you have a series, as your ad dollars stretch farther. Same with print books. The revenue to you is higher on a $14.99 book in Amazon than typically the $3.99 or $4.99 book, making it easier to absorb ad costs.

How to analyze your publishing business using the ARC method

How to use the ARC method to review the seven aspects of your publishing business.

Marketing

1. Who is your book written for?

2. Where do your readers congregate?

3. What methods are best for communicating to them?

Quality Product

1. Do I have a professionally created cover that appeals to people in my genre?

2. Is my book professionally edited?

3. Is my internal layout up to publishing standards?

Product Placement

1. Am I using the publishing model that best works for me? (Traditional, Indie, Hybrid, Vanity)

2. Where is your book currently distributed?

3. Have I maximized my keywords to increase my discoverability and visibility?

4. Do I need to work through a distributor or individual retailers?

5. Do you have a good book description on the product page?

6. Have I used all ten product categories available on Amazon?

7. Is my Amazon product page enticing?

8. Traditional Product Placement

    a. Am I maximizing all the formats available for my book? (Print, eBook, and Audio, graphic novel or screenplay)

Platform

1. What platform tool(s) am I currently using to extend and amplify my message?

2. Where am I visible on the internet?

3. What platform tool can I use to increase my engagement with my potential audience?

4. What new platform tools should I use, if any this year?

5. Do I have an email list?

Promotion

1. What free promotional tools am I currently using to increase my discoverability?

2. Do I have 20 reviews? If not, what promotional tools will I use to get them?

3. How am I tracking if the promotional tools I am using are working?

4. What promotional tools will I use in the next 90 days?

5. Where can you give your book away in exchange for an honest review?

Advertisement

1. What paid advertisement tools am I currently using to increase discoverability?

2. What is my current budget for advertising?

3. Which advertisement tool(s) will I expand to use within the next 90 days?

4. Non-traditional placement

5. Are there specialty shops that might be a good fit for my product?

6. Is there the possibility of placement of my book in airports, or libraries, in government commissaries?

7. Are there mass merchandise retail outlets that can be explored?

8. What are the options to place the book in schools?

5 places to get reviews

1. http://readindies.blogspot.com/p/get-featured.html

2. http://readersrealm1.wordpress.com/join-us/

3. http://soiinterviewedanauthor.blogspot.com/p/author-tips-and-faqs.html

4. http://fyreflybooks.wordpress.com/about/book-blogs-search/

5. http://www.bodyandsoulpublishing.com/?s=Blog+Tour+hosts+for+Christian+authors

5 Places to Get Discovered

1. Christian Authors On Tour

2. http://www.buzzblogger.com/600-places-to-share-your-content/

3. http://readindies.blogspot.com/p/get-featured.html

4. http://readersrealm1.wordpress.com/join-us/

5. http://www.ebookbooster.com/

How to develop connections online

4 resources about free giveaways

1. http://hbspublications.blogspot.com/2013_05_01_archive.html

2. How to get Great Amazon Reviews for Your Brand New Novel–Pretty much, what it says. This post explains the difference between good reviews (from legit readers) and

critical reviews (paid for, from family members, etc.) then dishes out a sweet strategy for securing some great reviews for your new book.

3. Why I'm All in with KDP Select – One writer's reasoning behind why he's choosing to distribute his eBooks only through Amazon in order to take advantage of their KDP Select program which makes certain marketing tools (like free book giveaway days) available for authors.

4. KDP Select Still Works in 2013 (or How My Novel was Downloaded 17,000 Times in 3 Days) – A follow-up to "Why I'm All in with KDP Select", this post documents the authors' experiment using Amazon's KDP Select.

Suggested ways to make connections and engage

Authors today are bombarded with several choices when it comes to publishing. Traditional publishing options, indie publishing, hybrid publishing, etc. However, one thing remains clear. Your platform comprises people that you have connected to.

Common advice is not to spam people with "buy my book." on social media and to make actual connections. Sometimes, for us introverted authors that can be as challenging as trying to self-edit your own work.

Author Kristin Lamb in her book Rise of the Machines: Human Authors in a Digital World. Talks about the need to make connections with people and summarizes the persons that authors need to connect with. It is a splendid book and one I highly recommend for indie authors.

I believe that you have to actively go to make connections, and typically, when I do it, I look at three things.

1. What do I have that is of value to another? (Knowledge, resources etc.)

2. And where can I find those who can use that knowledge and resources

3. I am looking last at what the other person has, that might be of value to me. And sometimes wondering, can I mentor from them? Can I tap into their knowledge?

Overall, when I go online, I try to spend some time at least weekly simply looking at whom I can help advance in their authorpreneurship. This does not mean that I have it all together. It also does not mean that I am NOT looking to learn from others. (In fact, just the opposite is true. I find that the more I share, the more I learn.)

It means that my aim is to give my knowledge and resources away. As a Christian, I believe you reap what you sow and that said act of generosity will, at some point, return.

So let us walk through how you can use this strategy to build relationships online and, subsequently, your own platform.

First, go on your favorite social media platform: I use those Facebook and Twitter where I am the most active.

Look for groups where you can take part. You are looking for writers' groups in general and groups in your genre in particular.

When you join the groups, spend some time reading the posts and learning the culture of the group. Learn what is ok and what is not ok. Who are the moderators and how do they handle group problems? This is important, as you do not want to violate any group norms. It is best to introduce yourself by saying hello, thank them for allowing you to join, and let them know you want to be a positive contributor where you can.

Now comes the key part. Look for posts where people are asking for help.

I find that when I go into a group, there are two types of posts: those that are information sharing and those from individuals looking for help. The latter posts you really want to zero in on.

Once you find a "can you help me post?" Then do your best to answer the question the person is asking.

I would not suggest giving snarky remarks or general information; give a specific "how to" on how that person can get what they want. Give a link if you know an online resource.

Only answer questions you really know the answer to or have had experience. Remember, you want to give away your knowledge or resources. (A resource, by the way, can be an author interview: allowing them to guest blog. A book review tweeting something for them on your platform: anything that might raise their own visibility and or advance them using your means to do.)

Remember, the goal is to be extremely helpful. Do not answer questions the person has not asked. Do not presume that they do not know other things. Just stick to answering the question they raised in the group. If you are not clear about something, ask them privately, if possible, with a direct message.

Let's recap.

1. Go online, at least, weekly, with the purpose of helping solve someone else's problem

2. Join writing groups and groups in your genre to help facilitate this

3. Introduce yourself to the moderators, learn the group's culture

4. Scan the posts of the group to find those persons who are looking for help

5. Answer their question with a specific "how to" do not give generic advice.

Here are some other tips.

1. Do not poo-poo other people's answers.

2. If a post has the answer you would have given, find another person to help.

3. Emphasize that this has worked for you. I.e., it is your subjective experience that helped get you what you were looking for. Its mileage may vary for others.

4. Always tell them you hoped that helps! In other words, be friendly!

5. Remember, every author is a reader and has a platform just like you. It may be small or large, but they have one. Be a help to others and you might find the favor returned.

How I APE'd my book.

U sing A.P.E. by Guy Kawasaki as a template, I will use his breakdown to show how I completed my first novel, the Third Heaven: The Rise of Fallen Stars. Kawasaki says that a writer has three hats when she self-publishes: Author, Publisher, and Entrepreneur. (i.e., A.P.E.) Each hat requires a distinct set of skills. Most writers are accustomed to the author hat, but to be successful as an indie author, you need to become adept at all three. Here is essentially how I "aped" my first novel.

Author

1. Hardware: I wrote the Third Heaven on various PC's and laptops.

2. Software: Scrivener & Microsoft Word, and Adobe InDesign. I saved countless versions to my email and off-site storage, so if something happened, I could recover my work. I am currently using Evernote to help me keep an online journal or catalog of things I need.

3. Reviewing: I had 7-10 beta reviewers read the material and incorporated as much of the suggestions that I thought added to the work.

4. I self-edited as best I could (for example; I used Microsoft Word's read text feature to read the novel back to me. That helped catch some errors.)

Publisher

Layout

1. I learned about proper layout design and did it myself. I used Adobe InDesign to layout the print version of the book and produced a print-ready PDF file that was sent to Lightning Source. The same PDF was provided to CreateSpace. I also used Fiverr.com the second go round, as it was easier.

2. For this book, I used InDesign to create the pdf and Createspace (Now KDP) to do the print version.

Cover Design

1. I used 99designs.com to gain my cover designer; Roger Despi for the Third Heaven series. For this book, I used the premiere membership of Authormarketingclub.com and found a cover that fit for this book. I purchased the eBook cover, then used a free template from / to create a general spine and back cover of this book as a template, then turned it over to Roger to create the final spine and back cover.

Professional copyediting

1. I used an editor (Adele Brinkley) I found on LinkedIn to do the final edits, paying her 500 dollars to do it. It took approx. 3-4 months to do. I also used Natalie Davis for a second edit of the same book. For the second book in my series, I used Natalie Davis exclusively. I found Natalie through a referral from a fellow author on Facebook. For the third book in my series, I used a fan who had editing experience.

Online resellers

1. I initially signed up for Kindle Direct Publishing, Smashwords, and Barnes and Noble. I have since backed away to just using Amazon's KDP and specifically their KDP Select program. When my fan base is larger and email list is larger than I will broaden to the other distributors using what's called the wide approach.

Print versions

I used both CreateSpace (Now KDP) and Lightning Source for the print versions of T3rdH. By using both printers it allowed me to be in the Ingram distribution system that brick-and-mortar bookstores used, as they tend to not want to purchase books from Amazon who is a competitor.

1. I completed the audio version with ACX.com after each print version was out

2. I acquired 10 ISBN's via Bowker

Entrepreneur

1. Blog Reviews. I did a blog tour with Virtual Book Tour Café

2. Acquired Amazon Reviews via (Story Cartel, soliciting bloggers in my genre, using Author Marketing Clubs tool to find emails and soliciting reviews who reviewed sim-

ilar books. Looking up for possible readers on Goodreads. LibraryThing's giveaway, Goodreads giveaways Asking in Facebook groups, and LinkedIn, friends who read it..

3. The book was promoted using my social media on Facebook, Twitter, and LinkedIn accounts.

4. Blog radio podcasts: I did four interviews total, one with the Christian Author Show, The G-Zone, http://www.blogtalkradio.com/gelatisscoop, Lynda Brown on the Author Chat Show, and with Parker J. Cole on Blog talk radio.

5. Traditional PR: I was featured on Livonia Life Magazine, and I did a non-paid press release on my own.

6. Advertisement: I have used Facebook and AMS ads to advertise. I have done many email promotions using Ereadernewstoday, Fussy Librarian and on other similar types of outlets.

Must own books

The following books I consider must-own reading and should be staples if you are serious about being an Authorpreneur. Each will give you an excellent understanding of the publishing industry and give you the background necessary to understand how to be successful in this business. They go into much more detail in their specific areas than what is intended in this book. These are not presented in any specific order.

Platform by Michael Hyatt

A.P.E.: How to publish a book by Kawasaki and Welch

Let's Get Visible by David Gaughran

Rise of the Machines by Kristine Lamb

Write. Publish. Repeat. by Sean Platt & Johnny B. Truant

Your first 1000 Copies by Tim Grahl

How to Make Real Money Selling Books: Brian Jud (Deals with non-traditional publishing.)

Mastering Amazon Ads by Brian Meeks

Write to Market by Chris Fox

Become a Successful Indie Author by Craig Martelle

Help My Facebook Ads Suck! By Michael Cooper

What I did then vs. now.

In doing a new edition of this book its important to acknowledge the multitude of changes that have taken place in the industry. As of this date we have things like Canva, AI(ChatGPT, Claude, Gemini, etc.) Atticus (the formatting software I am using to create the layout of this updated version of the book. We have tools like Scrivener, Prowriting Aid, 20books to 50k Facebook Groups, Midjourney, BookFunnel, Elevenlabs AI, and I could go on and on.

So the process that I use now to bring a book to market has changed.

With that being said, in using the same APE template, this is how I do things presently.

Author

1. Hardware: I still write on a PC and or laptops. I think hardware is less of an issue. It's about finding the method that works for you. (ipad, chromebook etc.)

2. Software: Scrivener & Microsoft Word, and Atticus. I save countless versions to my email and off-site storage, so if something happened, I could recover my work. (I save on backup drives all the time.) I do not recommend KDP's writing and layout program Kindle Create as when you are done you are forced into their exclusive format.

3. Reviewing: I try to obtain 7-10 beta reviewers to read the material and incorporate as much of the suggestions that I think adds to the work. Always account for people who will not beta read. People mean well but some don't come through for various reasons. Others actually will read the book but not give feedback. So it's important to get available, reliable people who will follow the feedback guidelines you need.

4. I self-edit as best I can (for example; I use Microsoft Word's read text feature to read the novel back to me. That helps me catch some errors.) Currently I use Grammarly, Prowriting Aid and MS Word collectively. I always recommend listening to the book via MS-Word's audio feature to hear if something is missing. Obviously if you can afford an editor I always recommend one.

Publisher

1. Layout

I do all my layout in Atticus. now. It's just so much simpler. If you have an apple computer use Vellum to layout your book.

2. Cover Design

Currently, I use both a human graphic designer and or AI to do my cover initial generation then go into Photoshop and edit it to taste. I will use Midjourney and or Ideogram to give me an idea of how the cover should look. I will still use my cover designer Roger Despi but if I need to go with another person I would definitely still go 99 designs as I like original covers, so I don't use pre-made anymore.

3. Professional copyediting

Now I just self edit using the three tools I mentioned earlier. Auto crit is a great tool for developmental edits, and or course with AI you have a myriad of tools to do developmental edits if you're comfortable using those tools.

4. Online resellers

Amazon. Nuff said.

5. Print versions

I used both CreateSpace (Now KDP) and Lightning Source for the print versions of T3rdH. By using both printers it allowed me to be in the Ingram distribution system that brick-and-mortar bookstores used, as they tend to not want to purchase books from Amazon who is a competitor.

1. I still do audio books less so with ACX now they just take so much of the profit. I am seeing how the industry treats AI narration as it has improved. I have toyed with putting audiobooks on my website and sell them directly, go wide on google books and Amazon and putting them on YouTube and monetizing the video. Also if you go with a narrator make sure you can contract for the whole series. Do it all at once not one at a time in case something happens and have a series having to do multiple narrators.

2. I still get my ISBN's from Bowker for major books I want under my own imprint. Smaller titles I'm fine with Amazon showing as the publisher.

Entrepreneur

1. I still attempt to touch base with bloggers for new books.

2. Acquired Amazon Reviews via (Story Cartel, soliciting bloggers in my genre, using

Author Marketing Clubs tool to find emails and soliciting reviews who reviewed similar books. Looking up for possible readers on Goodreads. LibraryThing's giveaway, Goodreads giveaways Asking in Facebook groups, and LinkedIn, friends who read it.

3. Use social media on Facebook, Twitter, and LinkedIn accounts etc.

4. I go to a lot more in-person events now. I find places where I can sell in-person. Also look at the author in grocery store program. https://authorsingrocerystores.com/

5. Advertisement: I use Amazon ads and plan to do Tik Tok videos.

Curated web resources

Author Writing Helps (Items dealing with writing, plotting, editing, and revision etc.)

- Tips about world building

    - writersdigest.com

    - **World Anvil:** A tool for building and managing your fictional worlds. (https://www.worldanvil.com/)

- Fantasy Name Generator

    - fantasynamegenerators.com

- How to keep your characters frustrated.

    - helpingwritersbecomeauthors.com

- Learn from Peter Jackson on doing epic battle scenes

    - insidemovies.ew.com

- Showing vs Telling

    - scribendi.com

- How to print out your scrivener index cards

    - quepublishing.com

- **Writing Craft & Structure:**

- ○ **Fictionary:** AI-powered story editing software. (https://fictionary.co/)

- ○ **One Stop for Writers:** A comprehensive library of writing tools and resources. (https://onestopforwriters.com/)

- ○ **Plottr:** Software for outlining and structuring your book. (https://plottr.com/)

- ○ **The Writer's Helping Writers® Toolbox:** Free downloads and resources on writing and editing. (https://writershelpingwriters.net/resources-for-writers/)

- **Character Development:**

  - ○ **Character Therapist:** A website to help you delve into your characters' psychology. (https://thecharactertherapist.com/)

  - ○ **One Stop for Writers® Character Development Tools:** Specific tools within One Stop for Writers for character creation. (https://onestopforwriters.com/character-development-tools/)

- **Editing & Revision:**

  - ○ **ProWritingAid:** Grammar and style checking software. (https://prowritingaid.com/)

  - ○ **BetaReader.io:** Reader and feedback management for authors. (https://betareader.io/)

- **Writing Communities:**

  - ○ **Alliance of Independent Authors (ALLi):** Offers a wealth of resources and a supportive community. (https://www.allianceindependentauthors.org/)

  - ○ **Scribophile:** Online writing community for critique and discussion. (https://www.scribophile.com/)

Publishing Helps : (Items dealing with layout and design)

- All about ISBN's: thebookdesigner.com

- Get help on laying out your books bergsland.org

- 10 Free places to promote you book!

  - angiesdiary.com

- Turning your book into a graphic novel?

  - thecreativepenn.com

  - nathanmassengill.com

- **Formatting & Design:**

  - **Canva:** Online graphic design tool for creating book covers and other visuals. (https://www.canva.com/)

  - **Reedsy:** Marketplace of vetted professionals for editing, cover design, and formatting. (https://reedsy.com/)

  - **BookBaby:** Self-publishing services including formatting and cover design. (https://www.bookbaby.com/)

  - **IngramSpark:** Self-publishing platform for print books. (https://www.ingramspark.com/)

- **Book Promotion & Discovery:**

  - **BookBub Partners:** For advertising and promoting books. (https://partners.bookbub.com/)

  - **Story Origin:** Cross-promotion platform for authors. (https://storyorigin.com/)

  - **BookFunnel:** Secure ebook delivery and email list building. (https://bookfunnel.com/)

  - **Prolific Works:** Ebook delivery and lead generation platform. (https://www.prolificworks.com/)

Entrepreneurial Helps: (Items dealing with legal, issues, reviews, marketing, promotion, exposure, discoverability etc.)
- A Tax Cheat Sheet for Kindle eBook Self-Publishing

- Publishers of Christian Speculative Fiction.

- Need places to review your book?

  - publishedtodeath.blogspot.com

  - storycartel.com

- How to make a website. Thanks to Hailey Dawn Stratton for the suggestion

  - sitebeginner.com

- Just write the next book is bad advice if no one knows about the first.

  - noorosha.com

- A place to get low cost net galley access

  - patchwork-press.com

- The best way to grow your platform

  - outthinkgroup.com

- How to format your eBook

  - blog.bookbaby.com

  - writeintoprint.com

- Keyword training

  - googleusercontent.com/youtube.com/2 (Note: This is a direct link to a YouTube video, which I cannot verify directly without opening the link. I've kept the original format.)

  - kdp.amazon.com

  - kdp.amazon.com

- Need to translate you novel to another language?

- translation-software-review.toptenreviews.com

- trainingauthors.com

- babelcube.com

- Where to get radio and TV interviews?

  - XXXXXXXX

- Overall goodies on making an audio book

- How ACX royalties work?

  - acx.com

- How to narrate your own book.

  - acx.com

- Submission guidelines

  - acx.com

- Great Info to help get an ad with Bookbub

  - indiesunlimited.com

- EBook Bargains UK is the world's first and currently only international ebook promotion newsletter. We send out daily newsletters to subscribers in fourteen countries / regions.

  - ebookbargainsuk.com

- Marketing options other than Bookbub

- Ebooksoda

  - ebooksoda.com

- Fussy Librarian

- thefussylibrarian.com

- ereadernewstoday

  - ereadernewstoday.com

- Kindle Books and Tips

  - fkbooksandtips.com

- A new way to do book promotion via phones

  - genrepulse.com

- Createspace Expanded Distribution vs Lightning Source what are the pros and cons?

  - newshelves.com

- Are platforms overrated for the indie author?

  - creativenonfiction.org

- 12 great publishing tools

  - thefutureofink.com

- Blog Review sites

  - docs.google.com/spreadsheet/pub?hl=en_US&hl=en_US&key=0ApH17IbfXGIXdHhJOVdYWDRjS1JRV1VUTFdiY2Z0Qnc&output=html

- Are Kirkus Reviews worth the price?

  - selfpublishingadvice.org

- Need international book translation?

  - babelcube.com

- A new way to acquire emails for your mailing list.

  - janefriedman.com

- hubspot.com

- How to increase exposure via LISTMANIA

  - howtoblogabook.com

- About author branding

  - jamigold.com

- Book conferences to go to that are African American based

  - aalbc.com

- Want a printer to print your comic?

  - ka-blam.com

- Great Facebook group to explore Graphic Novels

  - Facebook Group

- How to submit to comic publisher?

  - jasonthibault.com

- 10 great places to increase your discoverability

  - Goodreads: Giveaway your book (give 1 signed autographed copy)

  - Christian Author Show

  - KDP select

  - buzzblogger.com

  - authorspromotingauthors.org

  - blogspot.com

  - readersrealm1.wordpress.com

- bookblast.co

- ebookbooster.com

- mediabistro.com

- Here is an excellent resource to find sites to promote your discounted and free book. rachelleayala.com

- Locate the bloggers you need for reviews bookbloggerlist.com

- Need to know how to move from a free wordpress.com to a self hosted site? Here you go. wpbeginner.com

- Learn how to start an email list stevescottsite.com

- **Marketing & Promotion:**

  - **Smith Publicity:** Book marketing and publicity firm with resources for authors. (https://www.smithpublicity.com/)

  - **The Creative Penn:** Website and podcast with valuable marketing and publishing advice. (https://www.thecreativepenn.com/)

  - **Advanced Fiction Writing:** Website with marketing tools and tips for writers. (https://www.advancedfictionwriting.com/)

- **Author Website Platforms:**

  - **WordPress:** Popular and versatile platform for author websites. (https://wordpress.org/)

  - **WPEngine:** Managed WordPress hosting. (https://wpengine.com/)

  - **Thrive Suite:** A suite of WordPress plugins for marketing and website building. (https://thrivethemes.com/)

- **Legal & Business:**

  - **The Authors Guild:** Provides legal resources and support for authors. (https://

authorsguild.org/)

- **Iubenda:** Privacy policy generator for websites. (https://www.iubenda.com/)

- **Finding Agents & Publishers:**

  - **Duotrope:** Database for querying agents and editors. (https://duotrope.com/)

  - **QueryTracker:** Organization and information software for the agent search process. ([https://query

Thank You

T hank you for allowing me to share my writing with you. If you enjoyed this resource and have a moment to spare; I would appreciate a quick review on the page where you purchased the book. Your help in spreading the word is gratefully appreciated and reviews make a vast difference in helping new readers find it.

Also, feel free to check out my four-book speculative fictional series about the fall of Lucifer called the Third Heaven.

If you have the e-version of this book, press on the book cover to be taken to the web page! Otherwise check me out on Amazon.

Feel free to keep in touch with me on the following sites.

Email: tornveil@donovanmneal.com

Facebook: Donovan Martin Neal

X (formerly known as Twitter) @ Donovanmneal

About the Author

Donovan M. Neal is the Amazon best-selling independently published author of the Third Heaven Series: a speculative Christian fantasy four-book series that explores the captivating story about the fall of Lucifer.

Donovan has published twenty books. His books have reached thirteen countries including India, Japan, the Philippines, Mexico, Brazil, and across Europe, Canada, and the US. He has sold approximately thirty thousand units of his books without an agent. Donovan has produced fiction; non-fiction and most recently published a graphic novel. His genre of preference is fantasy and He has been named among such notable authors as Brian Godawa, Frank Perretti, and the late Dr. Michael S. Heiser.